SWOT Analysis

A Strengths, Weaknesses, Opportunities and Threats analysis a great tool to use for planning.

From business projects to self-improvement, SWOT is a fantastic tool that will help you to focus on your goals.

The SWOT format is designed to help you to specify the objectives you need to achieve in order to be successful.

A Typical SWOT chart is presented as a 4 square grid.
Each grid represents one of the elements of SWOT being the Strengths, Weaknesses, Opportunities and Threats that are applicable to what you are aiming to achieve.

Reading down the columns the relationship between Strengths and Opportunities
Is that these tend to be internal factors.
While Weakness's and Threats tend to be external factors.

Reading across the rows, the relationship between Strengths and Weakness is that you will aim to leverage Weaknesses into Strengths and Threats into Opportunities.

To complete the SWOT chart, mind storm with your team by or yourself to fill in each of the squares with relevant points.

Since the aim of SWOT is to help your progression towards your goals, there is no need for anyone not to be honest about his weakness's or foreseen threats.

It is in identifying these that you will become more productive and stronger in your tasks.

Soon, your Weakness's will become your Strengths and the Threats you will soon be able to leverage as your Opportunities.

This will help you achieve constant improvement in your life for your benefit.

Here is a sample SWOT analysis for a fictitious product release for a fictitious company.

There is a space above the SWOT chart for a title. Use this to help you to keep your goal in mind as you mind storm for ideas.

SWOT Analysis

1Dog Product Plan

STRENGTHS

[illegible]

WEAKNESSES

Upcoming competing products for main competitor.
Spending on luxury goods trending downwards.
Small margin of opportunity.

OPPORTUNITIES

Unmatched product placement.
Affluent target market.
Shallow learning curve needed for support team.
Strong marketing team.

THREATS

Aggressive window of opportunity.
Competitors products.
Investment budget is tight.
Product plan leakage.

The SWOT templates in this book will help you with your own tasks and projects.

Using SWOT you can become a better planner and clearer thinker.

STRENGTHS	WEAKNESSES
OPPORTUNITIES	THREATS

STRENGTHS	WEAKNESSES
OPPORTUNITIES	**THREATS**

STRENGTHS	WEAKNESSES
OPPORTUNITIES	THREATS

STRENGTHS	WEAKNESSES
OPPORTUNITIES	**THREATS**

STRENGTHS	WEAKNESSES
OPPORTUNITIES	THREATS

STRENGTHS	WEAKNESSES
OPPORTUNITIES	**THREATS**

STRENGTHS	WEAKNESSES
OPPORTUNITIES	**THREATS**

STRENGTHS

WEAKNESSES

OPPORTUNITIES

THREATS

STRENGTHS	WEAKNESSES

OPPORTUNITIES	THREATS

STRENGTHS	WEAKNESSES
OPPORTUNITIES	THREATS

STRENGTHS	WEAKNESSES
OPPORTUNITIES	**THREATS**

STRENGTHS	WEAKNESSES
OPPORTUNITIES	THREATS

STRENGTHS	WEAKNESSES
OPPORTUNITIES	THREATS

STRENGTHS	WEAKNESSES
OPPORTUNITIES	THREATS

STRENGTHS	WEAKNESSES
OPPORTUNITIES	THREATS

STRENGTHS	WEAKNESSES
OPPORTUNITIES	THREATS

STRENGTHS	WEAKNESSES
OPPORTUNITIES	THREATS

STRENGTHS

WEAKNESSES

OPPORTUNITIES

THREATS

STRENGTHS	WEAKNESSES
OPPORTUNITIES	THREATS

STRENGTHS

WEAKNESSES

OPPORTUNITIES

THREATS

STRENGTHS

WEAKNESSES

OPPORTUNITIES

THREATS

STRENGTHS	WEAKNESSES
OPPORTUNITIES	**THREATS**

STRENGTHS	WEAKNESSES
OPPORTUNITIES	THREATS

STRENGTHS

WEAKNESSES

OPPORTUNITIES

THREATS

STRENGTHS

WEAKNESSES

OPPORTUNITIES

THREATS

STRENGTHS	WEAKNESSES
OPPORTUNITIES	**THREATS**

STRENGTHS	WEAKNESSES
OPPORTUNITIES	THREATS

STRENGTHS

WEAKNESSES

OPPORTUNITIES

THREATS

STRENGTHS	WEAKNESSES
OPPORTUNITIES	**THREATS**

STRENGTHS

WEAKNESSES

OPPORTUNITIES

THREATS

STRENGTHS	WEAKNESSES
OPPORTUNITIES	**THREATS**

STRENGTHS

WEAKNESSES

OPPORTUNITIES

THREATS

STRENGTHS	WEAKNESSES
OPPORTUNITIES	THREATS

STRENGTHS	WEAKNESSES
OPPORTUNITIES	THREATS

STRENGTHS	WEAKNESSES
OPPORTUNITIES	THREATS

STRENGTHS	WEAKNESSES
OPPORTUNITIES	THREATS

STRENGTHS	WEAKNESSES
OPPORTUNITIES	THREATS

STRENGTHS

WEAKNESSES

OPPORTUNITIES

THREATS

STRENGTHS	WEAKNESSES
OPPORTUNITIES	**THREATS**

STRENGTHS

WEAKNESSES

OPPORTUNITIES

THREATS

STRENGTHS

WEAKNESSES

OPPORTUNITIES

THREATS

STRENGTHS

WEAKNESSES

OPPORTUNITIES

THREATS

STRENGTHS	WEAKNESSES
OPPORTUNITIES	**THREATS**

STRENGTHS	WEAKNESSES
OPPORTUNITIES	**THREATS**

STRENGTHS	WEAKNESSES
OPPORTUNITIES	**THREATS**

| STRENGTHS | WEAKNESSES |

| OPPORTUNITIES | THREATS |

STRENGTHS	WEAKNESSES
OPPORTUNITIES	**THREATS**

STRENGTHS	WEAKNESSES
OPPORTUNITIES	**THREATS**

STRENGTHS	WEAKNESSES
OPPORTUNITIES	**THREATS**

STRENGTHS

WEAKNESSES

OPPORTUNITIES

THREATS

STRENGTHS	WEAKNESSES
OPPORTUNITIES	THREATS

STRENGTHS	WEAKNESSES
OPPORTUNITIES	THREATS

STRENGTHS

WEAKNESSES

OPPORTUNITIES

THREATS

STRENGTHS

WEAKNESSES

OPPORTUNITIES

THREATS

STRENGTHS

WEAKNESSES

OPPORTUNITIES

THREATS

STRENGTHS

WEAKNESSES

OPPORTUNITIES

THREATS

STRENGTHS

WEAKNESSES

OPPORTUNITIES

THREATS

STRENGTHS

WEAKNESSES

OPPORTUNITIES

THREATS

STRENGTHS

WEAKNESSES

OPPORTUNITIES

THREATS

STRENGTHS

WEAKNESSES

OPPORTUNITIES

THREATS

STRENGTHS	WEAKNESSES
OPPORTUNITIES	THREATS

STRENGTHS

WEAKNESSES

OPPORTUNITIES

THREATS

STRENGTHS

WEAKNESSES

OPPORTUNITIES

THREATS

STRENGTHS

WEAKNESSES

OPPORTUNITIES

THREATS

STRENGTHS	WEAKNESSES
OPPORTUNITIES	THREATS

STRENGTHS	WEAKNESSES
OPPORTUNITIES	**THREATS**

STRENGTHS

WEAKNESSES

OPPORTUNITIES

THREATS

STRENGTHS

WEAKNESSES

OPPORTUNITIES

THREATS

STRENGTHS	WEAKNESSES
OPPORTUNITIES	THREATS

STRENGTHS

WEAKNESSES

OPPORTUNITIES

THREATS

STRENGTHS

WEAKNESSES

OPPORTUNITIES

THREATS

STRENGTHS

WEAKNESSES

OPPORTUNITIES

THREATS

STRENGTHS

WEAKNESSES

OPPORTUNITIES

THREATS

STRENGTHS

WEAKNESSES

OPPORTUNITIES

THREATS

STRENGTHS

WEAKNESSES

OPPORTUNITIES

THREATS

STRENGTHS

WEAKNESSES

OPPORTUNITIES

THREATS

STRENGTHS

WEAKNESSES

OPPORTUNITIES

THREATS

STRENGTHS	WEAKNESSES
OPPORTUNITIES	**THREATS**

STRENGTHS	WEAKNESSES
OPPORTUNITIES	THREATS

STRENGTHS	WEAKNESSES
OPPORTUNITIES	THREATS

STRENGTHS	WEAKNESSES
OPPORTUNITIES	**THREATS**

STRENGTHS	WEAKNESSES
OPPORTUNITIES	THREATS

STRENGTHS	WEAKNESSES
OPPORTUNITIES	**THREATS**

STRENGTHS	WEAKNESSES
OPPORTUNITIES	THREATS

STRENGTHS	WEAKNESSES
OPPORTUNITIES	**THREATS**

STRENGTHS

WEAKNESSES

OPPORTUNITIES

THREATS

STRENGTHS	WEAKNESSES
OPPORTUNITIES	**THREATS**

STRENGTHS

WEAKNESSES

OPPORTUNITIES

THREATS

STRENGTHS	WEAKNESSES
OPPORTUNITIES	**THREATS**

STRENGTHS	WEAKNESSES
OPPORTUNITIES	THREATS

--------------		---------------
STRENGTHS		WEAKNESSES
OPPORTUNITIES		THREATS

STRENGTHS

WEAKNESSES

OPPORTUNITIES

THREATS

STRENGTHS	WEAKNESSES
OPPORTUNITIES	**THREATS**

STRENGTHS

WEAKNESSES

OPPORTUNITIES

THREATS

STRENGTHS

WEAKNESSES

OPPORTUNITIES

THREATS

STRENGTHS	WEAKNESSES
OPPORTUNITIES	THREATS

STRENGTHS

WEAKNESSES

OPPORTUNITIES

THREATS

STRENGTHS

WEAKNESSES

OPPORTUNITIES

THREATS

STRENGTHS	WEAKNESSES
OPPORTUNITIES	THREATS

STRENGTHS	WEAKNESSES
OPPORTUNITIES	**THREATS**

www.ingramcontent.com/pod-product-compliance
Lightning Source LLC
Chambersburg PA
CBHW080229180526
45158CB00008BA/2316